Love
AND
Its Horizon

Emmanuel LADOUCEUR

Copyright © 2020 by Emmanuel LADOUCEUR.

All rights reserved. This book or any portion of it may not be reproduced or used in any manner whatsoever without the publisher's written permission except for the use of brief quotations in a book review.

Printed in the United States of America.

First printing, 2020.

Contact the author at emmanuelladouceur.com

Love And Its Horizon

Dear readers,

Thank you very much
for paying for your tickets
to travel with me into this breathtaking world.
I believe that love is a beautiful world
in which you can find
your own beauty of survival,
the essence of your life, the spring of your family,
and the business of value.

In LOVE AND ITS HORIZON,
you will embrace love as a world of peace,
happiness, salvation, perfection,
change, prosperity, and progress,
instead of sadness, isolation, pain, or suffering.
It's all about love in all and all in love.

I sympathize with anyone in the world who has lost family members or friends during the lifetime of the evil CORONAVIRUS.

Sincerely,
Emmanuel LADOUCEUR, author

Contents

PART I: Love 9

PART II: Love Still 35

PART III: Love in All 49

PART IV: Love and Love 99

PART V: Verses about Love 139

Acknowledgements

I thank God for holding his breath on me, keeping his presence in my life, and remaining my sovereign instance of love. I believe God could make no more excellent sacrifice than give his only begotten son to save my brothers' lives and mine. That's a priceless act of love. Besides, I praise God for my dear parents, my mother Ghislaine, and my father, Bergile LADOUCEUR, for their incredible love and sacrifice in my favor. Moreover, I thank God for trimming my world with the most beautiful rose that I have ever met, my sweetie Babara. I am very thankful that she is the book, where I learn about the power of love in a relationship and living together. My sweet Babara strongly inspired my motivation to write this love poetry and prose book. In addition, I appreciate all the ones who shared ideas or other kinds of support with me. A special thanks to my brother-in-law Patrick Nenfy Regis for his positive thoughts about love. Besides, I thank my sister Guerline Ladouceur, my brother JN Baptiste Ladouceur, my friends Hitler, Jill, the former Deputy Jean Edzer VALENTIN, Rev. Pastor Victor Isidore, and his wife Mercilia Isidore, my mother-in-law Celonne Colin, my brother-in-law, Amando, and former co-workers at Books & Books (MIA) or other places, family members, classmates, friends, and colleagues, collaborators in RCD-Haiti (www.rcdhaiti.com), and all the Saints and colleague musicians of the Jubilee Church of Jesus Christ, among others, for their breath of love. Moreover, I especially thank my friend, Dr. Daniel JOSEPH, for sharing ideas and a fantastic review of this book. Finally, I thank my former professor, Mr. Abelard Merites, for encouraging me and all other teachers or professors who have taught me in my lifetime.

Dedication

I devote this book to my sweetheart, Babara, my daughter, Christlove, my son, Godson, my dear parents, all family members, collaborators, friends, and readers.

Love
AND
Its Horizon

PART I

Love

With eyes everywhere,
here and there,
It may be like
the beam of the sun
on the silent ocean,
and a thirsty bird
on the horizon
of the sickened world;

LOVE AND ITS HORIZON

skimming the leaves
of the bountiful encyclopedia,
swaying through grasses
in all blue gardens,
diving in pools
and smiling oceans.

In the shadow of tenderness and wisdom,
dreams of various love ranges,
I long for appreciating
any generous providers
who can share the exact
meaning of love.

Should I say it?
I simply need to know.
Love is not the scriptures
drawn on a piece paper,
but the strongest, the deepest, the highest,
the greatest, the most powerful
and the most valuable thing
on the horizon of life.
Love is the almighty person
that nobody can see,
but who is above all
and dominates all nations.

Need to know

There may be sketches,
speeches, outlooks, or other leaves
pretending to define love;

L♡ve is…
L♡ve is…

However, love is the treasure that someone is unable to define while he or she cannot live without it.

Just like watering a small tree
on a vast land,
everybody needs to constantly
cultivate love,
make it grow and bounce,
like blooming beautiful flowers,
even on the ruined wall
of the summer breath.

                                                  Love needs care

Besides anything else,
love is being consistently happy
when having a chance
to care for other people,
especially the ones who are in need.
Living with love must be feeling excited
about serving oneself and others well.

Love defines love,
through love and in love.
Love is the expression
of the heart where it is born.

Love is neither
the noise of the storm
nor the silence of the grave.
It is the blessed melody
of the lovers' heart,
which fertilizes
all barren land.

LOVE AND ITS HORIZON

Some people embrace love,
others cuddle infatuation.
No matter how you taste it,
love is love;
infatuation is infatuation.

                                                               Love is love

It's like the raindrops,
the number of approaches
about love.
However,
considering its infinite breadth,
it is still undefined
because no one
can draw its dead-on painting.

                                                   Love is undefined

Lovers should not shackle love
on the easy say,
"I love you;"
they must reveal it
through continuous action,
verbal affirmation and other
relevant languages,
which are critical
for the survival
of the relationship.

Someone may spend a long time
parroting love as reading an essay,
but without related feeding actions,
it's like a leader killing his nation
with sweet, but tricky words
and thorny roses in the palace
without exertion.

                                       Love is not limited to a say

Love is undefined,
but love is defined
in the one you love,
and who loves you.
Love is a universe
that nobody can measure.
If someone can know
the dimension of God,
he can also know
the width of love.

                                              Love is unmeasurable.

You mean love
for the one you love,
and who loves you.
The one you love,
and who admires you,
is the portrayal of love for you.

God means love.
He sent his one and only Son
to die for his people.
Then, anyone who loves God
must love his brothers and sisters,
and be ready for living
sacrifices.

                                                Love requires sacrifices

LOVE AND ITS HORIZON

Who can define love?
I don't know,
but I need to know.
I believe only Love
is smart enough
to do that job.
"As love is, love is."

People are unable
to decide
what love is.
They may puff a myriad
definitions on its bowl,
but only love defines love.

Thank you father,
God of all gods,
for being love,
and all what we need
to live a fortunate
life of peace,
freedom,
prosperity
and happiness.

In love, there is everything we need to live

LOVE AND ITS HORIZON

When I think about the sacrifices
my parents made for me,
I believe they love me so much, and I feel it.
I wonder what I can give as a reward to satisfy them.
I may give them anything I can,
but I believe there is nothing
that can cover the price they paid
to save my life and make me
the person I am today.

Before all, I believe love,
along with respect, is the first thing
I need to offer them,
besides anything else I should do
to show recognition of their love for me.
I can't forget how much my mom
suffered during her pregnancy to
give birth to me. I can't forget how hard it was for my
dad to take care of my mom
while she was sick after delivery.
It was just the beginning...

> My parents, WOW!

Love is the best flier of all. It flies higher than everything.

The one you love
is the beach
of your emotions.

If you shape your love
with truth, actions,
affirmative words,
commitment, whispers
and trust, among other services,
You will be able to continually
avoid evil crevices
and build a very successful
long-lasting relationship
with your partner.

LOVE AND ITS HORIZON

Sometimes you trend love
with your eyes tied only on sex
or biological attraction.
Love is not to sexually
sweeten yourself only.
There is more in this universe
to live a beautiful life.

                        Love is more than simply having sex

Love doesn't exist
simply for physical seduction,
or money-making,
but it embraces all.
It is the horizon that we need to
nurture and nurture constantly
to enrich our world.

LOVE AND ITS HORIZON

Don't love only for seeming beauty;
go deeper and listen to your heart.
Love has a countless dimension;
it's a force that no one can break.
However, its performance can be different
when reciprocity is mute.

Love can break any evil chain.
Love is the most powerful sword.
It can kill everyone's beats;
and any evil hook that prevents a person
from living freely.
Love is the ability to die within oneself
and live with the one you love.

LOVE AND ITS HORIZON

Love speaks in silence.
It is quiet in noise,
but it dances in music.
Love watches while in the dark, and smiles,
even in anger.

PART II

Love Still

It's like moving me out of jail
when you decide to forgive me.
I am entirely wrong;
I overlook the profound value of our existence and
essence that we sincerely blend.
I quit for no fault on your side.
I squandered my time
and I wasted much money;
I didn't think about how much
you were suffering from my infidelity.
I saw myself as if I was a prince,
appointing most ladies as queens,
but I fell into a dark world.

I emptied myself in vain; I thought they loved me,
but they only loved my money;
I feel ashamed, honey.
Despite all, you forgive me,
and you're ready to help me fill my emptiness
I believe God has used you to save me
I need to serve and praise him until I die.

                                      Sorry, darling!

LOVE AND ITS HORIZON

Love smiles all the time;
in the morning,
in the afternoon, in the evening, and at night,
even when there is no light.

Love produces love; love respects love.
Love lives because of love;
love can water love,
but lack of love can dry up love.
Love grows in the land of love,
and it flourishes on the tree of love.

                                                              Love feeds love

Love stands through the stands of love,
sings with the voice of love,
dances the melody of love,
speaks with the tongue of love,
looks with the eyes of love,
thinks with the mind of love,
and loves with the heart of love.

LOVE AND ITS HORIZON

Love touches with hands of love,
hears with ears of love,
smells through the nose of love,
blesses with the soul of love,
saves with the spirit of love,
lives a life of love,
and dies where there is no love,
even though love never dies.

Nothing is better than love.
Keep it alive and savor it
in your friendship,
your family,
your business,
your everything.

Without a touch of love in their lifespan,
the richest man and woman in the world
would feel misfortune and misery.

There is no wealth without love

It's not a mystery,
but a reality;
people drive several miles,
go through oceans and seas,
and fly to anywhere
simply for love.

Love always smiles;
love
always
smiles;
love never stops smiling.

Love is the food
that helps an empty couple
avoid the flood
of hunger,
and the breath
that makes lovers stay alive,
or resurrect from death.

LOVE AND ITS HORIZON

Love is not blind,
but love doesn't see
even though it sees everywhere.
Love is not deaf,
but love doesn't hear,
while it hears from everywhere,
and understands
even the silence
of the graveyard.
Love is not silent,
but it is quiet.

Love is like the bright sun
shining the day of lovers,
the crystal moon
enlightening their night,
the pure water
quenching their thirst
and the healthiest food
satisfying their hunger.

Lovers should not care
of head shakers,
naysayers,
tattlers,
and gossipers
because they are super killers.

                                                          Be careful with outsiders

Lovers!
Make your Love feel comfortable
on the table,
savor your nourishment,
enjoy your beauteous moment;
and work for your little paradise,
while opening your eyes
for a green life together
should be a common concern.

PART III

Love in All

As love is a golden key to success,
we need it in everything.
I'm not talking about craziness,
but love, love, and love.

                                                   There is no success without love.

Without love, passion, and dedication,
there may be no progress in a business;
if the owner(s) along with
the managers have no love
either for the industry,
the customers,
or the associates,
the company is likely to dive
into the pool of failure.

Business owners
should build and promote
the beach of love
for their customers
by investing in courtesy,
as the main rule
for the business
on the whole.

LOVE AND ITS HORIZON

There should be the existence of love
to greet Guests
with a smiling face
and warm
Regardless of the nature of the business,
it is crucial to make the guests feel at home
while being in the business district.
No matter what kind of business you are running,
It should be like using the rosemary
to attract and catch bees.

There should be a love
that understands gUests
and is ready to serve them.
All businessmen and businesswomen
need wisdom and understanding
to give satisfying help
to the customers
and to grow their businesses.
They must always be ready
to serve guests
with a spirit and an expression of love.

LOVE AND ITS HORIZON

There should be a love
that can explain to guEsts,
talk to them
and answer any challenging questions
they may encounter.
The guests are the people
of the business
and the business depends on them.
Be courteous with your customers
because courtesy is the right leader
for a successful business.

There should be a love
that can suggest
new items to gueSts;
and maximizes sales.
With a face of love,
on both offline and online,
you can make them feel comfortable,
and eager to add to their table.

There should be a love
that thanks to the guesTs,
automatically invite them back
and even inspire
friends or family members
to come to your business
instead of going to another one.

If you want to make progress
and success in your business,
please, be a loved and lovely G.U.E.S.T. to your Guests.

GUEST

A leader without love
is a leader on
the cliff of failure.
Successful leading
requires love
to motivate followers.
And leaders need love
to achieve their goals
by influencing others
to perform actions
in the right way.
Being serious and responsible
doesn't mean being out of love;
instead, it is a condition of love.

Great leaders are change-makers;
and making change requires love,
passion, dream, vision, and dedication.

Leading

The process of teaching
can't be successful without love.
If a teacher or a professor
doesn't like either the teaching
or his students,
he is likely to fail.
Teaching is not like grabbing a pie.
It requires knowledge, love,
preparation, motivation,
energy and passion.
If the teacher does not care about the students,
he won't be able to motivate them to learn,
he may kill their previous motivation,
and is more likely to drive them
to failure instead of success.

Love is a pass for success
in the learning process.
It sets readiness to learn
with effectiveness.

If you are a teacher,
please, don't feel you succeed
simply because you do something
and you get paid;
you need to think about
how effective you are
in motivating your students
on learning
to be successful in their careers,
mainly through your course.

Love in learning

In the teaching-learning process,
love is the key to success.
Without an atmosphere of love,
the students will not feel comfortable,
and they may stay out of the table
while the professor or the teacher is working.

Are you a teacher or a professor?
If yes, tell me how passionate you are
for the success of your students.
How do you engage them
during class time?
Do you let them participate?
Do you explain them enough
to help them understand what you are doing?
Do students like your class?
How do you motivate them to learn?

Teaching and learning without love
and dedication is an embrace of failure.

Sometimes, you look crazy
because you are crazy
for someone you love;
you feel there is no one else,
you let yourself die
on and for that person,
you lose yourself,
yet, he or she is like,
"Sorry for your loss."

                        Unshared love in a couple is very painful

LOVE AND ITS HORIZON

Partners must be respectful to each other;
respect is a famous stand
that keeps love on, and holds the lifespan
of the relationship.
Respect, commitment, trust, and understanding
are all couples' lifespan primary needs.

Jealousy is a devastating devil
that many people glamorize
considering it as a sign of love,
but it's a negative emotion
that stems from uncertainty and desire.
However, not everyone's jealousy
dances on the scene at the level
to break the crowd.

Lovers should turn jealousy
into a desire for betterment, change
and progression in a positive way
with a positive attitude,
but not as an evil demonstration
to kill, mistreat, or destroy.

How regrettable is this? Listen.
I had a nice man;
he was very understanding; he loved me so much,
and he was always by my side.
I mistakenly listened to a gossiper
who plotted to make me lose my bread.
She told me my husband was cheating,
and she proposed me a rich man
who said he loved me and who was ready
to give me a lot of money and properties.

I suddenly broke up with my husband.
It's like I was blind.
Worried about missing the boat,
I divorced out of my mind.
A friend had told me not to quit,
but I thought she didn't love me.
Instead, I broke with her too. When I met the new man,
I thought I grabbed the hidden treasure,
but ...Shame on me. He used me, and he emptied me
for nothing back. He had no respect for me at all.
I wish I had kept my man,
the man of my dream, instead of embracing the evil offer.

Poenitet

I am sorry
because I broke up my household blindly.
My husband had planned to invest with me
for the growth of our relationship and family,
but I was crazy for the hot money,
which has burned me body and soul.
Now, I am paying for my meanness.
I wish I had reasoned. I wish I had.
Is he ready to forgive me?
I need to know, I am afraid of a second...
Anyway, I learn a lot from that mistake.

Friends,
don't sell the beauty and the essence
of your relationship for a pie.
If you want to build
a serious partnership
and avoid remediless remorse,
don't risk being in love
with someone for or from whom
you don't feel a touch of love
even if he or she may possess the world.

If you don't have an emergency,
Don't force wearing the dress
that doesn't fit you
to avoid feeling ugly
all the time.

In a couple, love should exist on both sides.
If it is one-sided or unrequited,
it will not be productive;
the person who loves
will be suffering
like the slave of the hell.

                        Unrequited love leads to broken heart.

If you love someone,
and that person doesn't love you,
don't force anything
other than the loving
as the commandment of God,
to happen between you
and that person.
To be successful,
a love relation must be full of love
on both sides.

Reciprocal

Lovers must be serving
each other as servants,
but not as bosses.
They are retainers of each other.
Money is not the only need for a household.
If the man is making more money,
that should not mean he is the boss to mistreat;
If the woman makes more money than the man,
that shouldn't mean she is the boss.

If you help each other,
you are servants of each other.
The Bible says the man
is the chef of the woman,
but not the woman is the head of the man.
However, it doesn't mean the man has the right to
mistreat or abuse the woman, but to love, serve, and
care for her, as she has to respect, love, and care for her
husband. To assume that responsibility,
the man has to serve his wife with great respect, as
she has to show understanding, respect and love to her
husband in both usual and unusual circumstances.

LOVE AND ITS HORIZON

In the marriage,
the ideal couple never says,
"This is my money,
or this is your money,
but this is our money".
If you live together,
you should agree to work
to build a successful life in common.

With love, commitment, and a well-planned life,
couples can earn more money than expected
and bring wealth to the family.
"An ideal couple never plans
to stay idle and wither,
but to work and thrive."

Living with, "this is my money,
or this is your money is a killer,
but this is our money is a builder
for any married couple."
I don't point to a relationship that is out of
strapping stands, such as trust, honesty,
faithfulness, loyalty, respect,
responsibility, dream, vision
goals, and love.
I believe they are essential for building
a successful relationship.

Building trust is not a friend of
lying, cheating, stealing,
loathing, reclining,
disrespect, infidelity, dishonesty,
mistreatment and selfishness.
Trust is a sturdy bridge
of success for any relationship
which embraces it.

In some couples,
love exists
only before the marriage;
it is when everybody feels on edge
with the breath, the sweetness
the voice, the hands,
and the whispers of love.
But within the marriage life,
the breath of love is frozen.

LOVE AND ITS HORIZON

"Love is the incessantly
unavoidable strength
that can lead
to the success
of all households
and all engagement."

There is nothing
more beautiful
and more productive than love;
an amazing source
where life germinates,
grows,
produces,
provides,
and lives.

The presence of love
in a household
turns on
the button of life
on behalf of the family.

If you have children, are you a model of love for them?
Do you teach them about loving themselves
and loving others?
Do you know that love is the best nourishment
for your beloved children?
Can you think about how much your children
may suffer if they don't feel your love?
Would you imagine how much you cripple your
children when you don't make them feel your presence?
Do you know, besides God, you are the one to predict
the future of your kids? What kind of orientation do you
give them?
You may be working hard to take care of your children,
but do you set a time to embrace them and make them
feel like living?
How do you design and shape the future of your kids?
Consider yourself a child,
think about how much your parents' love counts for
you, and understand how vital your warmth is for your
child or your children.
Love is the best thing you can give to your children to
keep them growing alive.

Save your children

Lovers should live
like angels blessing
each other's soul,
and golden doves
caressing the leaves
of the tree of love
with whispers and
special breathing.

LOVE AND ITS HORIZON

Love is an infinite treasure
needed everywhere
for everyone.
Its government can govern
all nations on the earth at once
and give positive outcomes.

                                              Where love governs,
                                                  life reigns.

Love and trust
can't be separated;
they go together
as two indispensable
stands for the success
of any relationship.

Many so-called lovers
ignore what love is.

Many husbands or wives
ignore what love is,
what marriage is,
what a household is,
what an engagement is,
and what living together is.

There is no need to say
true love or true lovers,
except for reinforcement;
love is love,
and lovers are lovers.
True lovers are lovers,
but untrue lovers
are not.

Everybody needs to wear
the clothing of love,
which is the most beautiful,
the most valuable,
the most economical,
the most honorable,
the worthiest, the healthiest,
and the most potent tissue
someone can ever have to dress up,
and to be the most attractive
on both earth and heaven.

         Everybody needs love

Lovers should read
each other's book
to know each other better
and live as real lovers.
Lovers should learn
from each other
to better serve each other.
Lovers must be lovers,
but not killers;
I don't know,
any evil kind.

Your love must be the one
who hears you
when you don't speak;
your love must be the one
who feels you
when you don't touch;
your love must be the one
who kisses you
when he or she doesn't see your lips.

Love gives lovers
the readiness to
work,
talk,
dream,
think,
share,
invest,
organize,
pray,
worship,
spend,
save,
and live together.

This drawing portrays
love and lovers,
but not dealers,
either murders,
killers,
kidnappers,
thieves,
abusers,
or so-called lovers.

LOVE AND ITS HORIZON

Your love is the book
you read every day
when you don't see the scriptures,
the purchase you make
when you have no money,
and the gift you receive
when you are hopeless.

when there is no oxygen in the world,
your love is the air you breathe.

Love is the art of performing love.
It should include
unity,
understanding,
charity,
humility,
respect,
cooperation,
sharing,
forgiveness,
faithfulness,
fairness, justice
sincerity, loyalty, and trust.

Its scriptures must be
in loving letters
on the loving paper
of a warm heart.
There is no love without acts of love.

                                        The loving

LOVE AND ITS HORIZON

Please, open your eyes
and see the power of love.
Release your heart
with the spirit of love
and enjoy love.
Make love be
the necklace to your neck,
the scriptures of your book,
the steering wheel of your car,
the way of your way,
the breath of your lungs,
and the drum of your heart.

Love is an antibiotic that prevents all pathogens
from infecting human relationships.
Lovers need to keep inserting love chips, swiping, or
tapping love cards before they can successfully conduct
daily transactions.

Love is the art
that everybody should use
to decorate his or her world.
Some people pretend to love,
but their jars of love are full of emptiness.
Their love body is naked,
and their love heart is waving in the hollow.

Many so-called lovers
are out of love.
They waste the pure value of love,
pretending to fall in love
while doing evil things.

If everybody embraced love
through its dimension,
love would pour its blessings
on the entire world.

Don't stop loving your wife
because she fails many times;
Don't halt loving your husband
because he fails many times;
Don't abandon anyone
because of any repeated failures.
Failure is a path to lasting success.

Every time someone fails,
he will learn something new
that can better shape his behavior.
What a person learns from failure,
he keeps it for life.
If you never fail, you may be subject to a big failure,
unless it is a purpose of the invincible power.

                                                  Nobody is perfect.

Love is an ocean
where everyone should be able
to dive and swim with no fear.

It's dead painful
for partners to feel alone
while they are in love.

To build a loving partnership,
your passion should be
for the one you love and who loves you,
but not for the one who doesn't love you.
I know it's a struggle sometimes,
but you'd better avoid heading to the evil room
if you know it before.

However, Jesus requires us
to love everyone, including our enemies.
We do have to like everyone, but I believe that loving
people, in general, is different from being in love with
somebody with a promise of marriage
and living-together for life.
If you feel weak about your decision, pray to God
faithfully.
He is the one who can help you make the right choice,
and he will if you believe he can.

Many people deny love
and crush it.
It's like love doesn't exist
in their daily lives.
They ignore how much success love
can bring to their decisions,
actions, business, and life.
However, if all people loved with wholeheart,
life would be flourishing on the earth,
and everyone would be living in peace.
All wives,
husbands,
friends,
and collaborators would be the right choices;
and living on earth
would be like living
in heaven.

LOVE AND ITS HORIZON

There is a treasure behind living with love.

Please, love everyone;

You may not trust everyone

because not everyone is trustful,

but always do right to everyone.

"Love all, trust a few, do wrong to none."

-William Shakespeare, All's Well That Ends Well.

Love is not a friend of racism.

Love condemns discrimination,

hates torture and abuse,

and censures murder, or any kind of killing

Love stands for both black and white,

poor and wealthy,

healthful and sick,

single and married,

disabled or non-disabled,

kids, young, adults and older people,

orphans, widows, or couples, everyone.

Love is a big enemy of indifference;

Love is for all, and love cares for all.

Like blood, love keeps its unique color on everyone.

Everybody has the same right to love, to be loved

and to live until God takes his breath back.

Love for all, life for all

LOVE AND ITS HORIZON

With love, all lives matter.
The life of a black man
is as important as
the life of a white man.
The life of the poor
is as important as
the life of the rich.
Love vows justice for all consistently.

                                                          All lives matter

The Lover's Day is today
The Lover's Day is everyday
The Lover's time is now
The Lover's time is everytime
The Lover's Day is not only
That day
Known as Valentine's Day
That sometimes makes lovers unhappy
Because of misunderstanding
Of love and the loving.

The Lover's Day

PART IV

Love and Love

With the "I love you
and you love me,
heartedly married together,
not simply as a say,
but as both says and actions,
blessings will be
abundantly over your nation,
and your entire world will be blessed."

Mr. Bless and his lover are excited.
They have been in love for a couple of years;
they would like to stay in tune with love
and keep it as the basis of their lifespan together.

The lovers genuinely love their relationship and
enrich their love with commitment, respect, wisdom,
understanding, loyalty, trust, and healthful habits while
enjoying the fruit of their marriage.

The couple believes that love is the foundation
everybody should use to grow a beautiful family,
not for a specific time frame,
but until the breath leaves

To be successful in your relationship,
as partners, you should admit each person's uniqueness,
appreciate his or her value
and bear that everybody is unique.
Everybody has his features, customs,
strengths and weaknesses.
If you want to succeed in your relationship,
you should acknowledge all the above
and be ready to accommodate yourself with them.

Lovers should communicate consistently
and listen to each other.
Don't be the person to only say, but be also the person
to listen and to understand.
It is of great importance to live with empathy
and apply it in your relationship for good.

You cannot change a partner,
but God can help you make it a day if you are ready to
change yourself first, and constantly apply the rules of
love in your relationship and your entire life.

You mean a lot for your love;
you are the incarnation
of his or her decoration
and the quintessence
of his or her existence.
You are the light
in the darkness
of your loved one
and you are the fitness
in his or her clumsiness.

You are the reason
for the endless season
of your love,
you are the raw
on his (her) hollow,
and the keenness
in his (her) ineptness.

Please, listen,
"If you love me,
take care of me
while I am alive;
don't wait until I die
to give me a luxury coffin."

Love requires sacrifice and preparation for
change.
Don't forget it on the ice
because you need it
to succeed in life.
Love has power over the entire world;
If you travel to this universe,
it will bring change to your world.

Despite having partners,
some lovers feel lovesick;
some others feel good
because they follow the rules
of love every day.

"Many couples fail because they don't believe they can together."

LOVE AND ITS HORIZON

Don't be lazy;
do your best
to help each other
whenever needed.
Don't say you give money,
that's all.
Instead, talk to your partner,
cooperate,
and serve each other.
Love requires both
words and actions.

Be always positive,
read about each other pages,
work jointly on improvement,
Free yourself with love
and be successful.
Love with a positive attitude is the right way to
progress, happiness and success.

LOVE AND ITS HORIZON

Where love governs, life reigns.
Love opens the doors
for happiness,
joy, and prosperity.
It brings peace,
love and excitement;
it cleans dirty floors;
it changes the lousy attitude
and it gives betterment.

Where love governs, life reigns.
It gives hope,
honor, and admiration.
It creates attraction,
it leads to perfection (in the bible),
and it brings light
to the darkened heart.
It is a source of wellness,
mercy, and goodness.

Whoever you are, please love.
Love is a source of blessings
and prosperity that even the richest man
of the world can't purchase,
but everybody can freely have access to it.

A pastor or a priest may spend years preaching about love;
if he doesn't love his brothers and sisters, he does nothing.
The more you love others, the more others love you.

Lovers,
you should always maintain a positive attitude
and be passionate about the success
of not only your partner but also other people.

If love grabs and holds you,
you will not have hatred, betrayal,
or the kiss of Judas.
Instead, you will embrace love,
dedication, loyalty, frankness,
sincerity, harmony, and peace
as your driveway to success.

Love is steady
when lovers
apply its rules
in their together lives.
Love is always comely,
but not homely.
Let it haunt you
for a beauteous you,
and keep the right attitude
for a new you.

If you discover
the world of love,
you discover
the most significant thing
that has ever existed
in your horizon.

Dear father,
I don't have enough words
to thank you for the person
you are in my life and my family.
You are the light in my darkness
and the strength in my weakness.
You are love,
you mean love for me
and all your people.

I am very thankful
for everything
you have done in my favor.
You send your only begotten Son
on the earth to die for me
and my brothers and sisters.
What a sacrifice you have made
because you are love,
you mean love,
and you remain love.
Thank you, Lord, for your infinite love.

Heavenly Father

There is a secret in love;
whoever can reach it
will have life
boldly written for him,
and nobody will be able to erase it.

Victor Hugo said,
"Life is the flower
for which love is the honey."
I agree, but I also believe,
"love is the flower
for which life is the honey."

LOVE AND ITS HORIZON

Love and life are interchangeable
sources of flowers and honey
because where there is love,
there is life,
where there is life,
there is love.

Love invites us
to love our brothers,
and our sisters,
as we love ourselves;
it's a divine commandment.

As brothers and sisters,
sons and daughters of the same
father,
no matter what our nationality is,
no matter what language we speak,
no matter what amount of money
we may possess,
no matter what our color, race,
ethnicity, or generation is,
no matter what our ability,
or disability is,
we must love
and support one another.

"We all come to live
and we all come to die."

Let's love one another

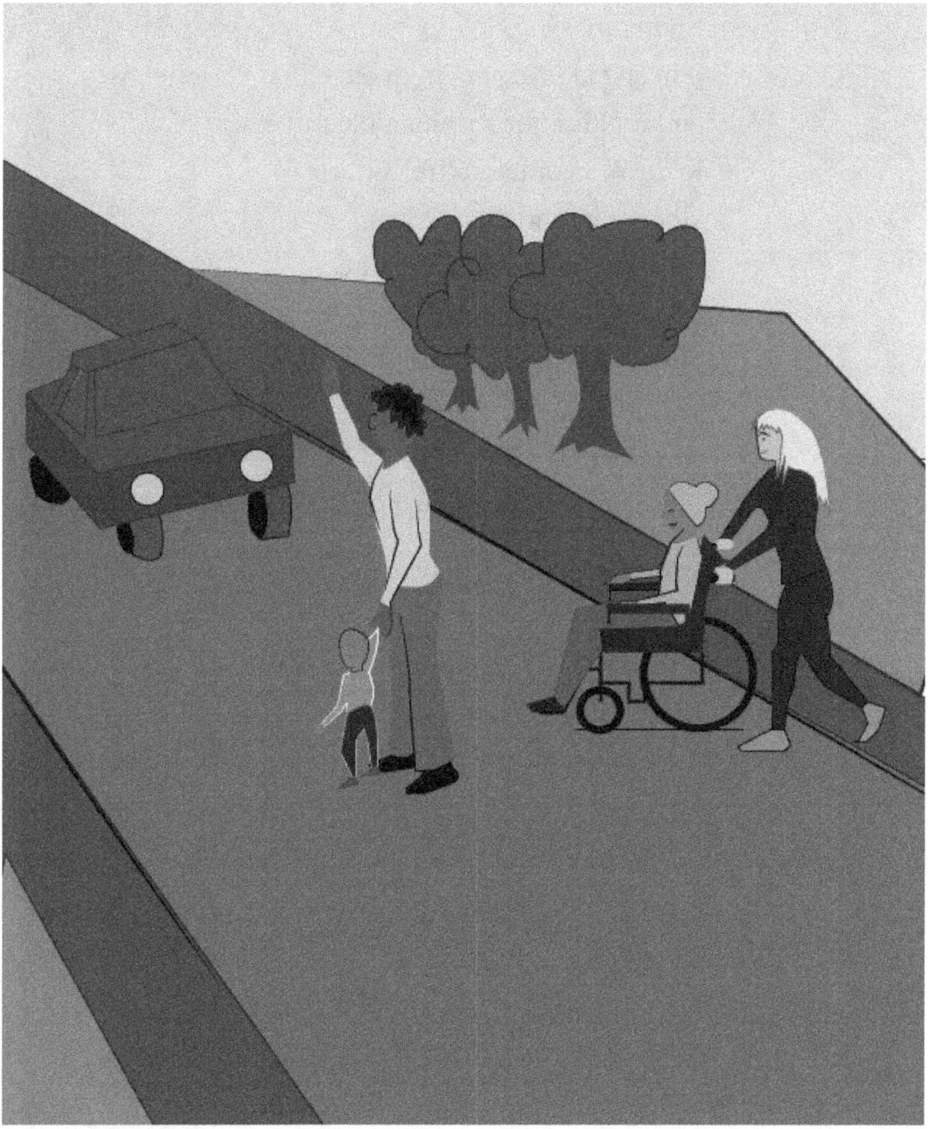

LOVE AND ITS HORIZON

Sometimes,
you spend years selling yourself
and looking for a romantic partner
to draw a common life culture;
when you find that person,
it's like the spring adventure
of a beautiful future.
However, after a few days together,
you discover the breaking
cartoon that keeps you
through its shiny picture.

The hurting

Not every partner is the right person
to fill your emptiness.
However, when something goes wrong,
you usually blame your partner,
but you rarely analyze yourself
while you may be the evil holder
abusing his rightness.

Check yourself first

Love is your shadow
when the evil heat
wants to break your window,
your shelter when the monstrous summer storm
wants to break your roof,
and your relief when pain wants to be your master.

Love is a treasure set for everyone,
but not everyone is smart enough
to grasp it and enrich his world.

LOVE AND ITS HORIZON

Love is the horizon,
or the behemoth
where life lives.
Love is the horizon
where life grows
and reigns.
People can fail,
but love will never fail;
love will always rule.

In both action and expression,
love must always be positive.
Lovers must avoid spitting evil slides on their partners
because actions and words shape the reality of any
relationship.

Love is not a friend of bitterness
and anger;
it contains sweetness and happiness.
It is a powerful source of light that can eliminate any
darkness,
and it can place liveliness in place of lifelessness.

LOVE AND ITS HORIZON

Lovers have to fight their indifference
to understand their differences
and get along with them to succeed in their
relationships. They may disagree on something,
but they should discuss their disagreement
with a positive attitude.
Lovers must avoid living with a grudge against each
other because this behavior is a powerful path to failure.
They must live with cordiality, comity and hospitality
for a successful lifespan together.

Nobody is perfect
in this world of diversity and perversity.
Everybody needs to acknowledge that each person is
unique with his nature and temperament.
Lovers need to know that they can't change a partner
in a day, but they can entail a progressive change with
love, tolerance, flexibility, and wisdom.
Love requires living sacrifices and patience.
The best way to help somebody change is to accept his
or her uniqueness and be ready to change yourself at
first.

Change yourself first

For a world of peace and freedom
without discrimination, corruption
and wars between countries,
we need love.

Love vows to clasp togetherness,
well-being, goodness,
rightness, happiness, peace, and success,
instead of isolation, ill-being,
wrongness, sadness, and failure.

         Love is the source of living.

Instead of wild jealousy,
love is trust and loyalty.
Love is not deception,
but integrity.
Go hand in hand
and give love
for joint success.

Love is the golden bridge
between black and white,
rich and poor
children, young and adults,
male and female.

> Let's do
> everything
> with love
> to beautify
> our world.

> Love is all
> what we
> need to live.

LOVE AND ITS HORIZON

Love doesn't mean
staying body-body
all the time.
As responsible lovers,
we all need a specific time
to shift in or out,
or to run a business
and to work on our goals;
but the button of love
should be always on
during both online
and offline on the zenith
of our daily wine.

Lovers should always consider creating
or doing something that can bring wealth
to the family rather than poverty or suffering.
They should ever dream of a prosperous family
and work together to reach that goal.

Understanding love

Love is the thinking,
the investing,
the growing,
the sharing,
the speaking,
the embracing,
the committing,
the sweetening,
the smiling,
the working,
and living together.
These are some of the pillars
of the wall of love.

Love,
I need you in everything,
everywhere,
and every time.
The light of my darkness,
you enlighten my world;
you make my daily wine
precious and delicious
with a divine flavor.
You are everything I need,
you are all in all.

                                                                  You are all in all

The alarm of change is ringing
that we hoist its flag
like a shining and waving art
in the breath of our hearts.
Even though I am not certain
about the color of my range,
I may fall between green and orange,
or others, painting the relief of my pain.

I want to change my world
for I can change the world;
let's turn our world
to change the world.
With love, we can make it.

                                            Love can make it

LOVE AND ITS HORIZON

I don't care if you lean
on Corinthian, Doric
or Ionic columns
to build your home.
It may be like a dome or other,
but we all need beautiful flowers
to trim our world.

There is a God of all gods;
he is the God of all architecture
and outstanding creatures.
He rules all countries
and the whole world.
He can break all evil mountains,
and help us swim in the ocean of love.

Taking love as the essence of life is
what we need to live together
in a dream world,
where there will be no killing,
no burning, no kidnapping,
no murdering, no shooting.

As creatures of the same father,
or sons and daughters
of God the Father,
we need to regard love
as the condition of living
and the foundation of our life.

The enlightening

Love says NO

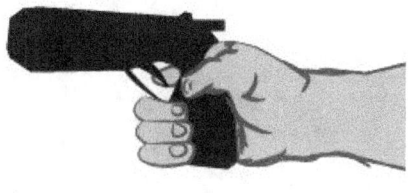

There is nothing more beautiful

than living with someone you love,

and who loves you.

My sweetheart,
when the angel came to me
while I was sleeping
to show me your angel pic,
I saw you by my side, but I didn't understand
despite he told me you were the one
I was going to marry.
I thought I had eaten too much
because we were not in touch at that moment.
However, the button of love was on
in our loving heart.

I didn't know you were waiting for me
even though the candle of my love
could burn you despite being physically apart,
and was burning you intensely.
I was swimming in your pool
and the warmth of your heart was watering me.
Even though I couldn't touch you,
and you couldn't touch me either,
we felt each other by listening
to the whispers of our hearts.

I didn't know you would be mine
I didn't take that revelation seriously
because you told me apart,
and we missed communicating
for more than two years after you left;
I didn't know it was the plan of God
that I marry someone to mean love
for me.

I thought I knew
the meaning of love,
in the living-together,
but I didn't know.
Honey, I feel free and happy
in the love garden
you created for me.
By living with you,
I breathe the air of your love all the time,
and I enjoy the warmth of your incomparable embrace.
You are exceptional, darling!

You are indeed
the one I need in my life.
I believe that God loves me so much
because you are part of me.
Among other things he does,
he creates you to beautify my life
and make me happy.
Apart from being my sweet wife, my dear,
you are my best friend.
Besides God, you are the essence of my life
and the reason for my excitement;
thank you for being the beauty of my existence.

I thank God for the two angels, he gives me
through your room,
our beautiful daughter, Christlove,
and our handsome son, Godson.
They are from an abundant source of love,
which entail them to pour love on you and me
all the time.
I am very excited about this beautiful family
we are, honey.

Without you in my life,
I could spend years looking on papers,
I wouldn't know what love means through the living-together because you are the one who means love to me.

God is love; he portrays everything related to love
but in our relationship,
and through our life together,
he uses you as a fantastic expression of love
that blesses me body and soul.
When I read on your shining face
your beautiful smile and your charming heart,
I see the meaning of love in bold.
I believe my adorable kids and you are part of the
demonstration of the love of God to me.
You are the one I need for life, honey;
thank you for being so special to me.

I love you, darling.
I cannot estimate the amount of love
I have for you. Love you so much, Bb.

My dream Sweetheart!

Thank you for loving me so much, Lord.
I am still alive because it is what you want for me.
There is no one else who can keep me safe during the lifetime of the evil CORONAVIRUS that kills more than a million people in the world.
In 2010, a catastrophic earthquake killed more than 220,000 people in Haiti; ten months after, evil cholera killed about 10,000 people;
I was there, but you kept me safe. I feel sorry for all the ones who are gone, but...No words.

I am not better than them, but my God has kept me on the scene to testify his greatness. Wow!
Thank you for your infinite love, God.
I still have your breath of life because you want that I continue living.
Again, I am not better than the people who died, or who are terminally ill, but you are lenient to me.
Thank you for your incomparable forbearance.
Lord, you deserve all my praises.
I promise to serve you until I die;
I will adore you until I pass away.
You deserve all my praises.

As David said in Psalm 103,
Praise the Lord, my soul;
all my inmost being,
praise his holy name.

I am wondering what I should do,
besides singing praises to God,
loving my brothers and sisters,
serving and worshipping God,
to show him my gratefulness
for his incomparable love.
I don't have enough words
to thank you, God, for your infinite grace;
Thank you for being so merciful
to me and my family.

My Jesus, you take the death,
and you give me life;
what's a price you pay
simply to save me.
It's more than a favor
I don't know what word
to use for it.
Please, Lord,
help me love my brothers and sisters
without condition.
I believe it's a perfect way
to make you happy with me.

                                            I praise you, Lord

PART V

Verses about Love

Love is patient
Love is kind
Love does not envy
Love does not boast
Love is not proud

(1 Corinthians 13:4)

LOVE AND ITS HORIZON

Love does not dishonor others
Love is not self-seeking
Love is not easily angered
Love keeps no record of wrongs

(1 Corinthian 13 v 5)

Love does not delight in evil
But rejoices with the truth
It always protects
Always trusts
Always hopes
Always perseveres

(1 Corinthian 13 v 6-7)

Let love be genuine
Abhor what is evil
Hold fast
To what is good

(Romans 12:9)

Love one another
With brotherly affection
Outdo one another
In showing honor

(Romans 12:10)

LOVE AND ITS HORIZON

Love is from God.
God is love
Whoever lives in love
Lives in God,
And God is in them.

(Ephesians 4:2)

Be completely humble
Be patient and gentle
Bearing with one
Another in love

(Ephesians 4:2))

LOVE AND ITS HORIZON

Above all,
Love each other deeply,
Because love covers
Over a multitude of sins.

(1 Peter 4:8)

Hatred stirs up strife, but love covers all sins.

(Proverbs 10:12)

LOVE AND ITS HORIZON

Love is patient,
Love is kind.
It does not envy,
It doesn't boast,
It is not proud.
It doesn't dishonor others
It is not self-seeking,
It is not easily angered,
It keeps no records of wrongs.

(1 Corinthian 13 :4-5)

Do everything in love.

(1 Corinthian 16: 14)

Let love and faithfulness
Never leave you;
Bind them around your neck,
Write them on the tablet
Of your heart.
Then you will win favor,
And a good name
In the sight of God and man.

(Proverb 3:3-4)

And so, we know
And rely on the love
God has for us.
God is love
Whoever lives in love
Lives in God
And God in them

(1 John 4:16)

My command is this:
Love each other
As I have loved you.

(John 15:12)

And now these remain:
Faith hope and love.
But, the greatest of these is love.

(1 Corinthian 13:13)

LOVE AND ITS HORIZON

*So now I am giving you
A new commandment:
Love each other.
Just as I have loved you,
You should love each other.
Your love for one another
Will prove to the world
That you are my disciples.*

(John 13: 34-35)

There is no fear in love.
But perfect love drives out fear,
Because fear has to do with punishment.
The one who fears
Is not made perfect in love.
We love because he first loves us.

(1 John 4:18-19)

For God so loved the world
That he gave his one and only Son,
That whoever believes in him
Shall not perish
But have eternal life.

(John 3:16)

Love must be sincere.
Hate what is evil;
Cling to what is good.
Be devoted to one another
In brotherly love.
Honor one another
Above yourselves.

(Romans 12:9-10)

LOVE AND ITS HORIZON

Love must be sincere.
Hate what is evil;
Cling to what is good.
Be devoted to one another
In brotherly love.
Honor one another
Above yourselves.

(Romans 12:9-10)

Above all,
Love each other deeply,
Because love covers over
A multitude of sins.

(1 Peter 4:8)

LOVE AND ITS HORIZON

If I have the gift of prophecy,
And can fathom all my mysteries,
And all knowledge,
And if I have a faith
That can move mountains,
But do not have love,
I have nothing.

(1 Corinthian 13:2)

My command is this:
Love each other
As I have loved you.

(John 15:12)

No one has ever seen God,
But if we love one another,
God lives in us,
And his love is made
Complete in us.

(1 John 4:12)

Whoever claims to love God
Yet hate a brother
Or a sister is a liar.
For whoever does not love
Their brother and sister,
Whom they have seen,
Cannot love God,
Whom they have not seen.

(1 John 4:20)

However, as it is written:
What no eye has seen,
What no ear has heard,
And what no human mind has conceived
  __The things God has prepared
For those who love him.

(1 Corinthian 2:9)

Let no doubt remain outstanding,
Except the continuing dept
To love one another,
For whoever loves others
Has fulfilled the law.

(Romain 13:8)

But the fruit of the Spirit is love,
joy, peace, forbearance,
kindness, goodness, faithfulness,
gentleness and self-control.

(Galatians 5:22)

Dear almighty God
Thank you so much
for being love for me and my family.
You cover me and you beautify my life with love.
I feel safe and I am safe
because of your presence in my life.
You hide my family and me
under your golden and infallible wings;
you are my bulletproof shelter
during all evil events and every time.

If I am still living
despite evil hurricanes, cholera,
storm, earthquake, ..., CORONAVIRUS
and other dreadful diseases, or viruses
that drive a ton of people to the grave,
It is just because of your love for me.
Please, help me love my brothers
and sisters more and more,
and keep serving and praising you endlessly.
I believe it is the best way
I can show you my gratefulness.

                                              Dear almighty God

About the Author

Emmanuel LADOUCEUR was born in Jacmel, Haiti, on March 3, 1984. The author worked in his homeland as a language teacher in many secondary schools and was the principal of a public high school named "Lycée de Musac," in La Vallée de Jacmel, Sud-Est, Haiti. Emmanuel co-founded a non-profit organization in Haiti, called in French words, "Rassemblement des Citoyens pour le Développement du Sud-est, Haiti, which stands for Union of Citizens for the Development of the Southeast, Haiti (www.rcdhaiti.com). Its mission is contributing to community development and supporting poor people, especially Orphans, older people, and people with disabilities. Moreover, Emmanuel is the co-founder of Baboowish LLC, the company, and the services ebizareas.com, bodyfittings.com, and emmanuelladouceur.com, focusing respectively on entrepreneurship and marketing, health and wellness, and self-growth. Emmanuel is living in Miami, Florida, with his wife, Babara, and his two children, Godson and Christlove. Emmanuel is currently majoring in business supervision and management at Miami-Dade College, specializing in accounting. Besides, Emmanuel is a tax preparer and a life insurance agent. Mr. Ladouceur likes reading poetry, personal growth, and business books. According to the author, love with a positive attitude and discipline is crucial for people to live a successful life.

Special Thanks and Request

Thank you very much for reading "Love and its Horizon." I believe this book will help you better understand love, the treasure, and the tool that can help you run a successful relationship, partnership, and business for a better life.

Please, do me a favor and write an honest and positive feedback on Amazon or any other site(s) where you may buy the book if it is possible. I will be excited to read your reviews and reply to any questions you may have wherever possible.

Thank you for reading "Love and its Horizon" and for encouraging me.

Sincerely,
Emmanuel LADOUCEUR, author.

"Love speaks louder than everything."

www.ingramcontent.com/pod-product-compliance
Lightning Source LLC
Chambersburg PA
CBHW071454080526
44587CB00014B/2108